CW01476682

All the Best!

WHAT SALES LEADERS DO!

The 22 Habits of An Effective Sales Person

JERRUND WILKERSON

WestBow Press books may be ordered through booksellers or by contacting:

WestBow Press
A Division of Thomas Nelson
1663 Liberty Drive
Bloomington, IN 47403
www.westbowpress.com
1-(866) 928-1240

ISBN: 978-1-4497-0227-4 (hc)
ISBN: 978-1-4497-0226-7 (e)

Library of Congress Control Number: 2010929635

Printed in the United States of America

WestBow Press rev. date: 05/27/2010

Contents

SUCCESS

... it begins now!

Acknowledgments

I'd like to thank the outstanding individuals I've had the privilege to work and associate with for teaching me sales leadership.

I'd also like to thank my family for their patience and support as I continue my journey of learning sales leadership.

Dedication

To Ms. Riley and BJ

Introduction

There are many books available today about selling. The primary purpose of *What Sales Leaders Do!* is to provide the reader with a simple, straightforward overview regarding the mechanics of the sales process and successful habits of sales people. They are the leaders.

Before the Call

Habit # 1

1. Expect to Be Successful

The sales leader approaches each customer with a healthy level of confidence and positive expectancy.

Perfection is not attainable, but if we chase perfection we can catch excellence.

—Vince Lombardi

Habit # 2

2. Have a Sales Call Objective

The sales leader has a clear understanding of what they want to accomplish during the sales call. There is a customer action objective for each call.

The most important thing about a goal is having one ...

—Geoffrey Abert

Plan of Action

Habit # 3

3. Calls on the Right Customers

The sales leader targets and calls on customers who are influential and can make things happen, rather than waste time calling on customers who:

- don't need their product
- who would not buy in enough quantities
- the sale would have little to no impact on total sales results
- won't be benefited by the product
- cannot afford to buy

Winning is not a sometime thing, it's an all the time thing. You don't do things right once in a while ... you do them right all the time.

—Vince Lombardi

Habit # 4

4. Plans Each Sales Presentation

The sales leader avoids carrying on pointless, rambling discussions that only waste time and lead nowhere (no objective).

The sales leader enters the world of the customer with a customer action objective. The same presentation is never given to all customers with a one-size-fits-all mentality.

An intelligent plan is the first step to success.

—Basil S. Walsh

Plan of Action

Habit # 5

5. Appreciates Customers Who Are Different

The sales leader understands that the "difficult" customer is likely indicating an interest in listening to the pitch with a desire to eventually buy their product or service.

The sales leader understands that the most pleasant customers, or the ones who seem to have all the time in the world, may not be the ones who will make a difference to the sales leader's bottom line.

Just because someone is abrupt doesn't mean it won't lead to a sale. The sales leader understands that often the reasons customers may appear difficult is because they are results-oriented and not interested in chitchat or wasting time.

Success doesn't come to you ... you go to it.

—Marva Collins

Habit # 6

6. Knows Competitive Information

The sales leader has sufficient and accurate information about the competitor's product and pricing and is able to make believable comparisons between their product and the competitor's.

Honesty is the best policy.

—Benjamin Franklin

PLAN OF ACTION

Habit # 7

7. Has a Planned Call Frequency

With most products, multiple sales calls are required to achieve the first sale and to maintain continued sales from an existing customer.

The sales leader understands this and arranges call frequency to target and see the high-potential customers with the right frequency to close the sale and maintain the business.

A good system shortens the road to the goal.

—Orison Swell Marden

Habit # 8

8. Works a Full Day

Since sales can be a numbers game, the sales leader understands that poor use of time prevents them from seeing as many customers as possible, resulting in lower sales.

Effective use of time is one of the biggest differentiators between a highly successful and an unsuccessful sales person. A sales leader will often work though lunch, be the last to leave for the day, and arrive on territory at the earliest reasonable time to see customers.

Nobody who ever gave their best regretted it.

—George Halas

Plan of Action

During the Sales Call

Once in front of the customer, the effective sales leader understands and knows how to execute on the basic selling algorithm:

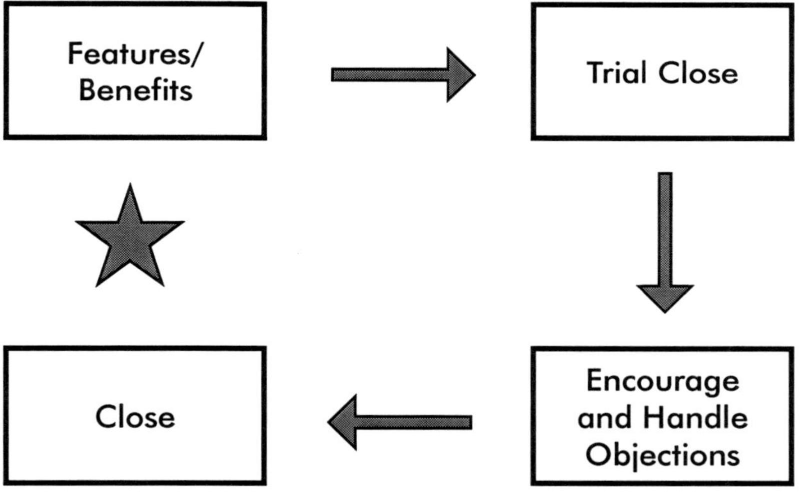

Habit # 9

9. Talks to the Decision-Maker(s)

To avoid wasting time with people with no buying power, the sales leader knows to verify whether the person receiving the sales pitch has purchasing ability.

Set priorities for your goals.... A major part of successful living lies in the ability to put first things first. Indeed, the reason most major goals are not achieved is that we spend our time doing second things first.

—Robert J. McKain

Habit # 10

10. Establishes a Connection/Rapport with the Customer

Once with the customer, the sales leader knows how to immediately assess the customer's interest and initiate conversation that engages/connects with the customer. The sales leader can then smoothly transition into the selling process.

If your imagination leads you to understand how quickly people grant your requests when those requests appeal to their self-interest, you can have practically anything you go after.

Napoleon Hill

Plan of Action

Habit # 11

11. Identifies and Establishes Customer Needs

The sales leader knows how to use questioning techniques to uncover the customer's need. Rather than focus on "selling," the sales leader concentrates on helping the customer "buy" through presenting features, advantages, and benefits of their product or service.

Here is a basic rule for winning success. Let's mark it in the mind and remember it.

The rule is: Success depends on the support of other people. The only hurdle between you and what you want to be is the support of others.

—David Joseph Schwartz

Habit # 12

12. Presents the Right Product

The sales leader only presents products that meet the customer's needs.

Things that matter most must never be at the mercy of things that matter least.

—Goethe

Plan of Action

Habit # 13

13. Uses Sales Aids Effectively

The sales leader always seeks opportunities to use sales aids in presentations. For example, even though information from printed material has been memorized, the sales leader uses sales aids to further establish credibility and increase customer retention regarding key points.

The sales leader memorizes the information, so they don't have to read it, therefore avoiding losing eye contact. The sales aids are used as a proof source to address the customers' questions or concerns and are then removed once the pertinent point has been made. The sales leader knows hearing and seeing information improves retention.

Retention: seeing and hearing information establishes a retention rate of 50+ percent.

—Cognitive Science, 13, 145–182, 1989

Habit # 14

14. Talks about Benefits

The sales leader knows the difference between a product feature and a customer benefit. The leader spends time talking about the relevant features of their product and always translates the features into customer benefits.

Always think in terms of what the other person wants.

—James Van Fleet

Plan of Action

Habit # 15

15. Allows the Customer to Respond

The sales leader holds conversations with the customer rather than gives speeches. Rather than trying to give a pitch and hoping something sticks, the sales leader encourages a two-way dialogue.

Take the trouble to stop and think of the other person's feelings, his viewpoints, his desires, and needs. Think more of what the other fellow wants and how he must feel.

—Maxwell Maltz

Habit # 16

16. Effectively Answers Questions about the Product

The sales leader is prepared with responses to commonly asked questions and/or concerns and when asked, provides relevant information.

They strive to avoid using the phrases such as "I don't know," "I'm not sure," "I'll get back with you," "Possibly," or "I think."

Success on any major scale requires you to accept responsibility.... In the final analysis, the one quality that all successful people have... is the ability to take on responsibility.

—Michael Korda

Plan of Action

Habit # 17

17. Handles Objections Effectively

The sales leader anticipates objections and sees them as a natural part of the sales process. They have gathered, studied, and become familiar with responses to the most common objections and/or concerns expressed by customers until they are no longer an obstacle to getting the sale.

It is true that you can succeed best and quickest by helping others to succeed.

—Napoleon Hill

Habit # 18

18. Does Things That Generate Sales for the Customer

The sales leader talks with all stakeholders to seek business needs and objectives to help develop a value-added interaction with the customer.

For example, for a selected product, build and monitor a business plan for the customer that generates an agreed upon revenue or accepted level and then work with the customers to ensure goals are met.

Customer service is not a department ... it's an attitude.

—Anonymous

Plan of Action

Habit # 19

19. Closes the Sale

A. Ask for the Business

The sales leader knows that a customer action objective requires asking the customer to do something at the end of the call . They know that the customer expects to be asked, to do something and asking for the business is an earned question, the payoff for all the hard work that preceded the question.

Sales leaders not only ask for the business, they ask for referrals, follow-up appointments, and introductions to colleagues.

If the sales leader does not have a customer action objective for the call, they will probably not ask the customer to take action.

B. Responds to Buying Signals

Sales leaders understand:

Buying signals are actions by the customer that indicate they are interested in purchasing the product. They are aware of buying signals and always prepared to move on them.

Some of the buying signals can be in the form of questions such as :

- "How much does this cost?"
- "Is it very expensive?"
- "Can I get this in ...?"
- "How long does it take to learn how to use it?"

The sales leader is prepared to answer all questions.

You'll always miss 100 percent of the shots you don't take.

—Wayne Gretzky

After the Sales Call

Habit # 20

20. Keeps Good Records of the Call

The sales leader keeps records of selling activities with the customer. Sales leaders can look at their customer records and recite the history of the selling progress per customer. The sales leader uses these records to connect calls with the customer for continuity, follow-up, and follow-through on sales opportunities.

Every situation, properly perceived, becomes an opportunity ...

—William Thetford

Plan of Action

Habit # 21

21. Analyzes the Sales Call

Following each call, the sales leader automatically analyzes and evaluates the impact of their customer call and objectively critiques what was done well and what is needed for improvement.

The sales leader measures the success of each call against the backdrop of their pre-call objective and the results/progress relative to the customer's action toward next steps. Based on the outcome analysis, methods used during follow-up calls are adjusted.

Most successful men have not achieved their distinction by having some new talent or opportunity presented to them. They have developed the opportunity that was at hand.

—Bruce Barton

Habit # 22

22. Follows Up

The sales leader is eager to respond to customer requests. The sales leader consistently seeks opportunities to establish partnerships with the customer. Once something is promised, they are committed to monitoring the follow-up to the customer's satisfaction.

A sales leader realizes one of the most effective ways to "sell" to a customer is to establish trust and credibility.

Giving people a little more than they expect is a good way to get back a lot more than you'd expect.

—Robert Hall

PLAN OF ACTION

Offer results, not alibis.

There are many people who—perhaps with the best of intentions—make promises they somehow never get around to keeping. These folks have usually developed a number of perfectly plausible explanations for not meeting their commitments; they have become experts at explaining away their failures.

Successful people, though, are those who accept responsibility for their lives. They know that talk is cheap; actions are all that really matter. The world is waiting for men and women who seek the opportunity to render real service-the kind of service that lightens the burdens of their neighbors, the kind of service that 95 percent of people do not render because they do not understand it. When you provide a truly useful service, enthusiastically and in a spirit of genuine helpfulness, success will automatically follow. The world seeks out such individuals and rewards them accordingly.

— Napoleon Hill

Overall Plan of Action

About the Author

Jerrund Wilkerson, RPh, MBA, is a senior business executive with more than twenty-five years of sales, management, and leadership experience. He is a business/organization leader, an entrepreneur and an educator in the area of leadership. Jerrund is a highly regarded and sought-after sales and leadership speaker.

Jerrund and his wife of more than thirty years, are the proud parents of three grown children.

CPSIA information can be obtained at www.ICGtesting.com
Printed in the USA
LVOW061014130112

263649LV00002B/1/P